*"Dear children,
let us not love with words
or speech but with actions
and in truth."*

1 JOHN 3:18

Dedicated to:

WE
THANK
GOD
FOR
YOU

1 THESSALONIANS 1:2

CHURCHLEADERS**PRESS**

WE THANK GOD FOR YOU
1 Thessalonians 1:2

Learn more at ChurchLeaders.com.

Credits
Contributing Authors: Gail Allyn Short, Janna Firestone,
    Christy Heitger-Ewing, Jessica Hanewinckel
Cover and Interior Design: RoseAnne Sather
Director of Content: Jennifer Hooks
Chief Operating Officer: Steve Foster
Chief Executive Officer: Scott Evans

ISBN: 978-1-958585-34-4
Printed in the United States of America by Outreach.

Table OF CONTENTS

You ARE LEAVING A MARK ON ETERNITY

Every early morning, every late evening, every time you step up when it would be easier to stay at home, you are making the world a better place. Whether it's extra hours, lots of elbow grease, or giving up your time, effort, and even pieces of your heart, you are an irreplaceable gift to God's family. You are one of the few workers in a harvest of plenty. You may not always see or feel the effects of your efforts today, but they have a ripple effect that touches many lives. By setting out chairs before the barbecue, you are saying, "You are welcome." By bringing food and clothing to the homeless under city bridges, you are saying, "You matter and God loves you." By replacing the roof on the church, you are saying, "This is God's house and we care for it." By serving as a small group leader, you are saying, "God sees you and He loves you." By greeting guests on Sunday mornings, you are saying, "We are glad you're here, and you matter to God."

This book is dedicated to all the volunteers who give of themselves for others. It's designed to offer inspirational stories, encouragement, prayer, reflection, and God's own words about serving others.

Your every act of service is a manifestation of God's love for us. Thank you for your heart for others, for your spirit of generosity, and for your faithfulness to God. ♥

A Prayer
FOR THE VOLUNTEER

Dear Heavenly Father,

The harvest is plentiful and the workers are few. Please guard your precious volunteers. Strengthen their hands and hearts. Give them stamina and help them find joy in serving Your people. Give Your faithful volunteers a sense of just how important they are to You and how You see their sacrifices and efforts to grow Your kingdom. Give them rest when they feel weary. Give them inspiration when they feel frustrated. Give them encouragement when they hit a brick wall or feel they can't go on. Let them know what a precious gift their labor and love is to You. In Jesus' name, amen.

*"In everything I did,
I showed you that by this kind of hard work
we must help the weak, remembering
the words the Lord Jesus Himself said:
'It is more blessed to give than to receive.'"*

ACTS 20:35

You are a beloved child of God. And it shows that you know it and live it each day. What you're doing week after week helps others see that they are beloved children of God, too. Each smile, kind word, welcoming look, and hour spent with others gives them a glimpse of His love for them. 💜

People who spend more than 100 hours each year volunteering are some of the most physically healthy people in the U.S.

SOURCE: AMERICORPS

Breaking Bread

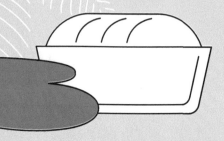

I n the early days of the COVID-19 pandemic, New Dover United Methodist Church in Edison, New Jersey, stopped in-person activities to prevent spreading the virus. But the church's congregants' desire to serve remained strong.

"We're surrounded by a lot of urban communities where there's need," says Pastor Chuck Coblentz. "But when the pandemic hit, the need became much greater. People from the church were saying, 'Hey, we can't come to church, but we want to do something. What can we do?'"

That is when congregant Brian Richards approached Coblentz with an idea: Make sandwiches for those in need.

Richards says he was inspired after talking with the head of a local homeless shelter. "I asked, 'What can we as a church do to support you?' And he looked at me and said, 'Sandwiches.'"

Coblentz named the church's new effort the Bread Breakers Ministry. Volunteers started out making around 50 sandwiches a week, but they quickly broke their own record.

"There have been weeks when we've made almost 1,500 sandwiches," Coblentz says. He estimates the ministry's total meal output since 2020 is over 100,000.

The ministry is still going strong. On Friday mornings, volunteers gather in the church's fellowship hall to make the sandwiches, from lunch meat and cheese to peanut butter and jelly. They place two sandwiches in each bag plus condiments. They also include side items like fruit cups, chips, and bottled water, paid for with donations.

Afterward, the lunches are delivered to several local nonprofits and people on the street. Bread Breakers Ministry volunteers include others besides New Dover members, Richards says. "We have Jewish friends who help us out. A mosque got involved. Amazing partnerships developed." For his part, Coblentz says he views feeding people as a spiritual act.

"We don't separate that from the spiritual aspect of the proclaimed Word. It's all connected."

You're more than what you do (which is a lot!). You're an image-bearer. God created you in His image and gave you specific talents to use to draw others to Him. And that's just what you're doing. So keep going. You're making a huge difference in the lives of others. ♥

When you think of yourself as an image-bearer, what comes to mind?

Feeding
THE CHURCH PLANT

A young man began attending a new church. He was new to the faith—asking lots of questions and learning quite a bit about what it meant to be a Christian. He quickly noticed that during church services, the pastor would often give updates on a church plant the congregation seemed very excited about. The church had recently begun raising funds for the plant, and the pastor gave weekly financial updates. "We need this money for the church plant," the pastor would say. "Let's keep supporting the church plant!"

After several weeks, the young man was completely confused. He contemplated the fundraising effort, wanting to join in all the excitement, but not wanting to ask silly questions.

WOW, he finally surmised. *That must be one* nice *church plant,* he thought, imagining a truly majestic specimen of potted foliage. 💜

"Carry each other's burdens, and in this way you will fulfill the law of Christ."

GALATIANS 6:2

Each time you give of your time and effort, you are doing a valuable, good thing. Not only are you meeting an immediate need, but you're doing so with the love of Jesus. Each person you encounter sees Jesus through you. And when you serve with love, you're drawing others close to Him, as well. 💜

What is one way you have relieved a burden for another follower of Christ?

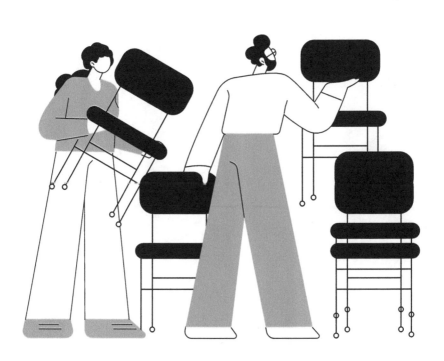

Getting **A WIFE**

A children's ministry volunteer was leading a preschool class in a series about Creation, covering one day of creation each weekend. During one of the final Sunday school lessons in the series, the teacher excitedly shared about the sixth day when God created man and woman. One small boy became especially fascinated when the teacher explained how Eve was created from one of Adam's ribs.

Later in the week, the boy's mother called to say she'd found him lying on the floor, holding his side and groaning. When she asked him what was wrong, his reply was priceless: "Mommy, I have a pain in my side! I think I'm getting a wife." ♥

About 35% of all American volunteers in 2021 said they gave their time to a religious organization.

SOURCE: GALLUP

A Vision
FOR MISSION

Back in 2001, the leadership team at Shades Mountain Baptist Church in Birmingham, Alabama, launched a vision plan that laid out lofty goals. By the end of 2010, they wanted to have people serving in all 24 time zones around the world. They strove to plant a church in every international mission board throughout their region. They aimed to do ministry in all 50 states, plus plant five churches in the U.S. and one church in Canada.

Ultimately, the church did ministry in 21 time zones, covered 15 regions, and planted seven churches in the U.S. and one in Canada.

"I tell people that my theology is better than my geography because there are three time zones in the Pacific Ocean where there's no one around, so it's difficult to cover those," jokes former Senior Pastor Danny Wood. Senior Pastor George Wright took the helm in 2021 with the church's vision in mind.

The vision plan, according to Wood, served to keep people focused on specific goals. By coming alongside the North American Mission Board, the church aligned from a strategic standpoint, supporting the planting efforts in those cities that were the least resourced and the

least served. The emphasis was for them to then reproduce indigenous church plants within that context.

"A lot of churches want to grow disciples and impact the community, but here we actually start with an action verb. We say, 'If you're going to be a part of this church, you need to know that we're about sending out,'" says Tim Wheat, pastor of missional living at Shades Mountain. It's a message of service that speaks to every demographic in the congregation, from older adults to kindergartners.

"The earlier you start, the more fruit you're going to produce," says Wood, noting that sixth-graders at the church go on a mission trip to Seeker Springs Ministry in Eros, Louisiana, to work with the impoverished. For many, it's their first mission trip, but it's far from their last. In fact, by the time they graduate from high school, these young people may well have gone on six to eight mission trips, some international.

"As a result, their whole view is so different from other college students who may have lived within the bubble of their community," says Wood, who adds that whenever missionaries visit the church, they are impressed with the questions Sunday school students ask about their work.

"[The kids] are integrated with all of this," says Wood. "They are already a step ahead when it comes to missions and thinking about how they can invest their life."

In 2017, the church laid out a new vision to take them to 2025. According to the North American Mission Board, there are 32 "sending" cities all around North America.

"We've got a goal to do ministry in all 32 of those cities and to try to find some partnerships with church planters there," says Wood. The church is working on connecting with unreached people groups overseas as well as on a Bible translation in Nepal. In addition, they are doing a lot of community mission work by adopting schools, ministering to first responders and helping with orphan and foster care.

In 2020 and 2021, COVID-19 forced church leaders and congregants to learn to go with the flow in every way, shape and form.

"Every plan we made was on an Etch-A-Sketch," says Wood. Despite the ever-evolving plans, people's spirits remained upbeat. Even when things were shutting down, Wheat says that directive to go with the flow became catalytic for them to mobilize people to serve in their neighborhoods.

"It really helped to move the needle of personal involvement in missions to a whole other level," he says. "It's about us influencing our world, bringing people into relationship with Christ and being sent out as disciples."

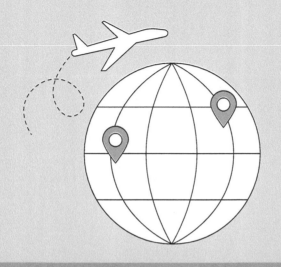

"Living by faith
includes the call to something greater
than cowardly self-preservation."

J.R.R. TOLKIEN,
AUTHOR

> *"This is a trustworthy saying.*
> *And I want you to stress these things,*
> *so that those who have trusted in God*
> *may be careful to devote themselves to*
> *doing what is good. These things*
> *are excellent and profitable*
> *for everyone."*

TITUS 3:8

You are so highly valued in this ministry. Or, to put it another way—important, treasured, dear, beneficial, cherished. We thank God that He chose you to serve in this ministry (and that you said yes!).

We thank God for you. ♥

23

Serving IN THE DEEP END

B eing vulnerable in ministry is risky. People are broken. Confusion happens. Feelings get hurt. Serving can be hard work with long hours. There can be conflict with leaders and other volunteers.

But it's so worth it to "give yourself fully to the work of the Lord." Sure, there will always be hiccups along the way, but when you're serving in the "deep end," you can't help but get a little wet. You get to experience the aha moments when kids in your class grasp a new concept. Or the joy that comes when volunteers quickly become dear friends. Or the satisfaction of seeing a life improved or even changed.

God blesses you deeply when you give of yourself deeply. He gives your work eternal purpose as you serve as the hands and feet of Jesus. Your work matters, and your work lasts a lifetime. 💜

People who volunteer have a 40% lower chance of developing high blood pressure. SOURCE: AMERICORPS

"Stand firm. Let nothing move you. Always give yourselves fully to the work of the Lord, because you know that your labor in the Lord is not in vain."

1 CORINTHIANS 15:58

"*Therefore encourage one another and build each other up, just as in fact you are doing.*"

1 THESSALONIANS 5:11

One key benefit of serving in ministry is your own faith growth! Various studies have reported that volunteers say they experience a deepening personal faith through the act of serving others. That's because serving is a central component of a maturing faith and personal understanding of Scripture. Serve to grow, grow to serve! 💜

> "I give all the glory to God.
> It's kind of a win-win situation.
> The glory goes up to Him,
> and the blessings fall down on me."
>
> GABBY DOUGLAS,
> AMERICAN GYMNAST

Old Spokes HOME

Retired policeman Harold Nuefang had a unique holiday tradition: Each Christmas, he would distribute used bicycles he had fixed to children in need. But when the Tacoma, Washington, resident died in 2000, no successor stepped up to continue his legacy.

That changed when a group of Marine View Presbyterian Church volunteers decided to revive Nuefang's charitable giving through an effort they called Bikes for Kids.

"Our small group decided, 'Hey, we could take that on,'" says Don Cowan, Bikes for Kids co-director. "But we knew nothing about [fixing] bikes."

Their lack of knowledge didn't deter the volunteers. With tutoring from former bicycle repairmen, the group met their goal of refurbishing 100 bicycles in time for Christmas. By 2015, the Bikes for Kids crew had ballooned to 30 volunteers, and Marine View Presbyterian had supplied the ministry with a former manse that they converted into a bike shop.

> *"Each of you should use whatever gift you have received to serve others, as faithful stewards of God's grace in its various forms."*

1 PETER 4:10

Bicycle donations come in from individuals, recycling events, and area bike drop-off locations. To raise funds, the team will sometimes sell some of the donated bikes at the annual Tacoma Bike Swap event.

Expanding its team and forming partnerships with other charitable organizations gives the Bikes for Kids program the capacity to refurbish and distribute hundreds of bicycles. To date, the team has taken in 14,374 bikes, with some of them salvaged for parts and others sent to recycling. They distribute the bikes to people in the community through partner organizations.

Including Cowan, most of the volunteers are retirees who feel a sense of purpose through their participation in Bikes for Kids. About half do not attend Marine View Presbyterian Church but simply want to repair bikes for children in need.

"It's been a good outreach in terms of getting other people involved," Cowan says. "It's about giving back. It's about being part of something that is bigger than ourselves."

LOVE. GRACE. ENCOURAGEMENT. HOPE. STRENGTH.

These are all things we need for ourselves each and every day. And we can't fabricate them on our own. We can find short-term substitutes. A good friend can speak a word of encouragement. A parent can love you. A mentor can help you find the strength to tackle the next day. But each of these can fade.

The same is true for our body's need for vitamin C to help fight sickness, serve as an antioxidant, and other helpful roles. Vitamin C is essential—meaning our bodies cannot make vitamin C on their own. We need to obtain vitamin C from food sources. And since our bodies cannot store vitamin C well or for very long, we need a regular intake of vitamin C.

Likewise, while you're serving others, encourage them. Give them hope. Love them well. But don't stop there. Connect them with the True Source—the eternal source—of love, grace, encouragement, hope, and strength. 🩵

Nearly 96% of volunteers reported that serving others gave them a richer sense of purpose in life. SOURCE: AMERICORPS

"*May our Lord Jesus Christ Himself and God our Father, who loved us and by His grace gave us eternal encouragement and good hope, encourage your hearts and strengthen you in every good deed and word.*"

2 THESSALONIANS 2:16-17

"*The LORD tends His flock like a shepherd:
He gathers the lambs in His arms
and carries them close to His heart;
He gently leads those that have young.*"

ISAIAH 40:11

The *Good* SHEPHERD

Our God is a loving shepherd. God is always at work, each and every moment. Sometimes it's hard to believe it, especially when we're struggling. But did you notice the action verbs in this verse?

Tends Just as a shepherd makes sure his lambs have food, water, and protection, God tends to each of us. He is the ultimate provider of everything we need physically, emotionally, and spiritually.

Gathers While God doesn't literally gather His followers in a sheep pen, He does work through circumstances that draw us closer to Him. In this way, God gathers us in His arms.

Carries God, as our Good Shepherd, sees and knows exactly what we're going through. There's nothing that goes unnoticed by Him. And especially when we're struggling, He carries us.

Leads A shepherd knows the best and safest way for his sheep to travel, and the same is true of God. His way is best, and He leads us by His Word, wise and godly counsel, and the Holy Spirit as our guide.

Especially as you serve, you can trust the Good Shepherd to tend to you, gather you to Himself, carry you, and lead you. 💛

Communion **JUICE**

A small church, like many churches, used grape juice instead of wine for Communion. About once each month, the team in charge of Communion would prepare all the elements of the service for the rest of the congregation. Well, on this particular team, a well-meaning—and highly frugal—Communion team member purchased cases and cases of grape juice when it was on sale. After all, it was a great deal and helped stretch the Communion budget. Quite a bit of time

had passed and the grape juice supply was still strong. The team prepared for another Communion service. But after distributing wafers and juice cups, they noticed congregation members started having unusual reactions when they drank the juice. The churchgoers themselves were quite surprised as they took sips that Sunday morning, raising their eyebrows in wonder at the potent, fermented juice. 💙

"Put God first in everything you do …
Everything that I have is by the grace of
God, understand that. It's a gift …
I didn't always stick with Him,
but He stuck with me."

DENZEL WASHINGTON,
ACTOR

COOKING UP *Hope*

Erica Hoffman found a way to serve the Lord and help others as a busy, full-time working mother of three by making and freezing ready-to-cook meals. Erica began doing this herself years ago. Everyone appreciated the convenience of premade dinners, so she decided to make a volunteer ministry out of it. She and others meet at Faith Lutheran Church in Spicer, Minnesota, every other month to make freezer meals that the pastors can take on home visits.

"When I went to pick up my grocery order, I was asked what I was doing with 15 chickens. I told the cashier I was a doomsday prepper," says Hoffman with a chuckle.

Volunteers typically make between 16 and 20 meals at a time that are ideal for a slow cooker or that can go from freezer to table quickly. The volunteers store the meals in the freezer at church along with directions on what dry ingredients are needed, if any. The group has prepared such meals as Italian sausage rigatoni, meatloaf, meatballs, salsa chicken, and chili and beef stew, each of which serve between four and seven people.

"Our pastors have said that the people are so grateful to receive a meal when something tragic happens—or when good things happen, like the birth of a baby—because that part of their daily life has been taken care of," says Hoffman.

The volunteers who prepare the dinners enjoy fulfilling that need, and all ages participate.

"We had a grandmother and her adult granddaughter come in to make meals together," says Hoffman.

When people sign up to make the meals, Hoffman assigns them to one of four groups, purposefully putting them with people they don't know so that new friendships can form.

"We've had some neat connections develop through that fellowship," she says. "It's a great way to get to know people from your church that you didn't know before." 💜

"*The LORD your God is with you,*
the Mighty Warrior who saves.
He will take great delight in you;
in his love he will no longer rebuke you,
but will rejoice over you with singing."

ZEPHANIAH 3:17

Our creative God gave us each incredible gifts. Some of us are great with numbers, while others are inspired by visual art and creativity. Still others are gifted in relating to people and making them feel special. God's great plan is for all of us—with our vast array of giftings—to come together with one purpose: sharing Him with others.

Just think of all the vital hearts and hands it takes for ministry to take place on Sunday mornings:

- Financial givers keep the lights on.
- Leadership provides the vision for the church and empowers those who serve.
- Parents get their kids ready and bring them to church.
- The cleaning crew ensures a tidy and safe environment.
- Sunday school teachers create space for children and adults to spend time with God and each other.
- Churchgoers faithfully get up, get ready, and bring themselves (and sometimes their baggage) in order to deepen their relationship with God.
- Leaders of volunteers manage schedules and behind-the-scenes logistics.
- Greeters welcome attendees and help fill their emotional buckets.
- Pastors prepare their message and minister to the flock throughout the week, often late into the night.
- Substitutes and helpers often save the day with their ministry of availability.
- And all the others who selflessly step up and serve in so many ways.

GOD IS SO CREATIVE. He chose you to serve in a vital role within the ministry. 💜

*"Just as a body, though one,
has many parts, but all its many parts
form one body, so it is with Christ.
For we were all baptized by one Spirit
so as to form one body—whether Jews or
Gentiles, slave or free—and we were
all given the one Spirit to drink."*

1 CORINTHIANS 12:12-13

Social isolation is a major issue for many older adults. Loneliness and limited interactions with others can negatively impact a person's health. Community involvement and especially volunteering are beneficial for this age group as they foster socialization and positive interactions. Studies show that individuals who volunteer tend to be less depressed than those who don't.

SOURCE: THE CORPORATION FOR NATIONAL AND COMMUNITY SERVICE

PAWS AND *Reflect*

D r. Nancy Moore understands that people can come to know Jesus just because they love their pets. She had taken mission trips with Christian Veterinary Mission (CVM) to visit Lakota reservations in Oklahoma and New Mexico. There, she treated animals whose owners couldn't afford veterinary care. While examining the animals, she shared her faith with the pet owners.

So in 2021, Moore approached Yerusha Bunag, local missions director of Idlewild Baptist Church in Lutz, Florida, to suggest the church volunteers could host an urban vet clinic. They chose their Sulphur Springs location, which is in a low-income neighborhood that doesn't have a veterinary clinic within a five-mile radius. The church supplied logistics and volunteers while CVM brought Christian vets, vaccines, and other resources.

"By teaming with a parachurch ministry like CVM, we extend the reach of what a local church can do," says Moore. "These pet owners see that compassion for an animal can show how God loves them."

Moore has had church members tell her that they were too scared to do something missional, but because they love animals, this outreach was a natural fit for them.

"The pet element opened all kinds of doors that we don't normally have," says Bunag, who notes that folks in the community are used to churches showing up with food and clothing, but veterinary care is unique.

"These people may never step foot in a church, but they love their pets," she adds.

"All walks of life came through the clinic," says Moore. "We met people who were saved, others who were saved but disconnected from the church, and others who only heard the gospel because of their pet. It was just such a blessing." ♥

*"Sell your possessions and give to the poor.
Provide purses for yourselves that will not wear
out, a treasure in heaven that will never fail,
where no thief comes near and no moth destroys.
For where your treasure is,
there your heart will be also."*

LUKE 12:33-34

Reflect on this Scripture. Where is your treasure?

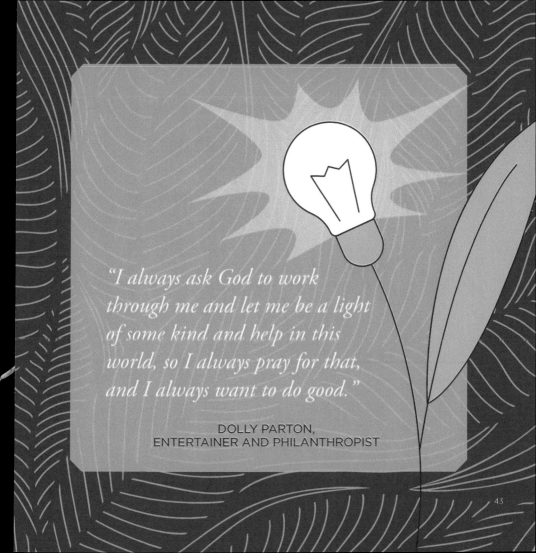

"*I always ask God to work through me and let me be a light of some kind and help in this world, so I always pray for that, and I always want to do good.*"

**DOLLY PARTON,
ENTERTAINER AND PHILANTHROPIST**

Love 'Em TILL THEY ASK WHY

At first glance, Living for the Brand Cowboy Church in Athens, Texas, was founded by cowboys, for cowboys. But, says Lead Pastor Frankie Smith, only about 20% of the church attendees are actual cowboys. The rest, he says, are folks from every walk of life. Living for the Brand aims to reach people through events held at the covered arena next to its main building. The facility is used for bull riding and rodeos, but it also hosts tractor pulls and car shows. Freestyle bullfighting events draw 1,600 to the arena. After one show, volunteers handed out church brochures as guests left. They also paused the show at one point to present the gospel, something the church does at every event it hosts.

"We want to stir up their curiosity enough that they'll come back on Sunday morning," Smith says.

The church is very community focused, holding a drive-through live nativity at Christmas with a raffle for a side of beef. Because the church is big on families, many events are geared toward kids, including bull riding for teens; Little Wranglers, an event that lets kids ride a horse, milk a pretend cow, "brand" goats with flour and a mop, and

> *"The one who plants and the one who waters have one purpose, and each will be rewarded according to their own labor. For we are co-workers in God's service; you are God's field, God's building."*
>
> 1 CORINTHIANS 3:8-9

barrel race with stick horses; and a special-needs kids rodeo.

Many in the church's leadership are actual cowboys, so they happily provide the animals, care, and expertise for events. But the heart of the church, Smith says, is sharing the gospel. "My heart is to see people have an experience that will create a relationship with Jesus. We're not here to build rodeo champions. We're here to build champions in life."

And whether church members are cowboys or not, that's something they can get behind and participate in. Everyone can love kids, love families, and love people. In fact, that's the church's motto: "Love 'em 'til they ask why." 🩶

God's Work **IN PROGRESS**

At a tour of a sculpture studio, guests were fascinated by the laborious process of creating a sculpture.

The local artist shared the arduous steps she takes in developing a sculpture. Extensive research begins the process. Then, experimentation and sketching help solidify a three-dimensional image. From there, the artist builds an armature and fills this structural frame with clay. After the artist completes the basic form of the sculpture, she cuts, molds, shapes, and texturizes the mound. And finally, the sculpture is cured and finished: a masterpiece.

God's process isn't all that different—though He could probably skip over the research. He already knows His creation: you. He knows how you're structured, and He's added substance underneath a changing exterior. And over time, God continues to shape you into who He created you to be. Experiences. Learning. Trials. Celebrations. Each aspect of your life provides depth and beauty. But it's not just for you. God created you—His masterpiece—as a gift to others. Each way you serve others, you're providing one more experience that's shaping them in return. ♥

46

"For we are God's handwork, created in Christ Jesus to do good works, which God prepared in advance for us to do."

EPHESIANS 2:10

Volunteering gives your mental health a boost.
Participating in meaningful and productive activities has a positive impact on the brain. It can also help you "feel happier and have a positive outlook on life."

SOURCE: NATIONAL INSTITUTE ON AGING

A *Welcoming* PLACE

On Sunday mornings, children, teens and young adults with developmental and physical disabilities gather to worship at the Rowen Glenn Center at Brentwood Baptist Church in Brentwood, Tennessee.

Named in honor of Brentwood Pastor Mike Glenn's granddaughter Rowen, who has disabilities, the center is a $6 million, 15,000-square-foot facility that serves 88 families in the Middle Tennessee area. The center, which opened its doors in January 2022, features classrooms, sensory rooms, interactive whiteboards, a kitchen, and even an indoor playground.

Jill Hartsfield, the center's programming director, says the facility offers caregivers a much-needed respite.

"We have parents who drop off their kiddos and go to a weekday Bible study and care for themselves, not only physically and emotionally, but spiritually, too," she says.

The church built the center to accommodate its ever-growing special-needs ministry, Hartsfield says. "The ministry grew from one classroom, one sensory room, and a buddy system to a full hallway. So then we had about four or five classrooms in the main part of the building."

In 2019, a benefactor made a donation toward expanding the special-needs ministry space. Other donations to build the center followed.

Besides Sunday services, the center also provides a weekday program for young adults featuring recreational and leisure classes.

In one case, a mother approached the center to ask if her adult son, who still wore diapers, could enroll. While other similar day programs rejected him, the Rowen Glenn Center welcomed him.

"It has been wonderful to see him blossom and have a place to go that's his own, apart from Mom," Hartsfield says. While not all day program students are Brentwood Baptist members, she adds, a few of them have started attending.

"It goes back to the parable of the great banquet in Luke 14 when the man goes out into the streets and invites the poor, the blind, the lame, and the crippled," Hartsfield says. "Obviously those aren't words we use anymore, but it's welcoming people with special needs into the church. Our church." ♥

Have you ever wondered what God thinks? What He *really* thinks? You spend your time planning and gathering supplies. Whether 5 or 500 people show up, whether all the volunteers show up, whether the plan works, and no matter how many things go wrong, He delights over you, His beloved child. Truly. ♥

> "You don't have to be a brain surgeon
> to be a valuable person.
> You become valuable because
> of the knowledge that you have.
> And that doesn't mean
> you won't fail sometimes.
> The important thing is to keep trying."
>
> BEN CARSON,
> BRAIN SURGEON

A PLACE
OF
Rest

Take a housing shortage, add the high cost of existing housing, and it is no surprise that the number of homeless people in San Diego County is on the rise. Meridian Baptist Church, however, came up with a creative solution to offer homeless women a respite.

Located in El Cajon, California, Meridian Baptist had some land it wasn't using, so Senior Pastor Rolland Slade suggested building "sleeping cabins," 96 square feet of livable space that doesn't have a permanent foundation or running water but does have electricity. The idea was to provide a place of solace for women with children so that they can rest and refocus before transitioning to permanent supportive housing or long-term transitional housing.

Slade reached out to city officials, navigating the proper channels to handle zoning issues and other details. Thankfully, all parties involved embraced his vision. In April 2019, the church partnered with builder Amikas and social services provider Home Start to build six emergency sleeping cabins for women with young children.

"We want them to come here to rest for a bit before they have to start making decisions that will impact their lives," says Slade, who hopes that other area churches will follow suit.

"If 100 of the 1,700 faith community properties in San Diego County would build six emergency sleeping cabins, that would provide 600 cabins," he says. "That would impact the homeless population in the county."

Meridian Baptist's six-cabin village, which features calming landscaping, has a raised garden bed to grow vegetables. Residents have access to the church's kitchen in the fellowship hall as well as a shower trailer.

Slade thinks of the homelessness issue through the lens of the four men who brought the paralytic to Jesus in Mark 2:4 by lowering him through the roof.

"We don't know their names. We just know that what was most important to them was getting their friend in front of Jesus," says Slade. "I think that's what we're doing." ♥

Volunteering grows new friendships.
When you volunteer, you join a community of like-minded
people with similar interests. Not only does volunteering
benefit your brain, it also benefits your heart!

SOURCE: PRB.ORG

A Closing Prayer
FOR VOLUNTEERS

Dear Heavenly Father,

Thank you for the heart of this precious volunteer. Please wrap your loving arms around Your volunteers. Give them strength when they feel tired. Show them the fruits of their labors. Reassure them when they wonder whether their efforts have impact. Bless them for the gifts and treasures they have given to Your ministry. Let them never forget the enormous blessing they have been to our ministry.

In Jesus' name, amen.

WE ALWAYS
THANK
GOD FOR ALL OF
YOU
AND CONTINUALLY
MENTION YOU
IN OUR PRAYERS.

1 THESSALONIANS 1:2